THE POWER OF METAPHYSICS

A Change in Lifestyle in Just 27 Days.
Make Use of the Principles of Attraction and
Manifestation
(2022 Guide for Beginners)

Alger Jordan

Table of Contents

Introduction

A wise old farmer in an old parable went outside to enjoy the evening air. He took in the gorgeous moon as he peered out into the horizon. His grandson joined him outside as they both gazed at the moon. After a period of conversation, his grandson asked him the following. "Grandpa, what is the key to happiness?" The farmer whistled for his dog to arrive, and it arrived immediately. The farmer gestured toward the moon with his finger. The farmer gestured, and the dog's attention was drawn to the farmer's finger.

In response, the farmer said, "I was pointing to a gorgeous moon, but my dog focused on my finger." The farmer then turned to face his grandson. The majority of us act in the parable's dog's manner. Instead of focusing on happiness as it naturally exists, we have shifted our attention to what we think leads to it.

Nobody has ever existed who didn't try to find happiness. Although we might not be actively looking for happiness, we unconsciously are. We are predisposed from birth to pursue happiness.

Even those who commit suicide do so because they believe it would be less painful than continuing to live. We are hunting for happiness in all the wrong places, to paraphrase a well-known song.

We are hooked on attaining happiness by focusing on things while being clueless about their source, just like the farmer's dog. What things do we concentrate on in our quest for happiness? The list goes on and on.

Relationships, sex, money, our careers, status, power, alcohol, drugs, other people's acceptance, and so forth are the most common ones. In actuality, our attention can be directed toward anything that we can think, perceive, hear, touch, or taste. Anything phenomenal is something that you can imagine in your mind or sense with your senses. Since we have fantastic experiences of the world, this is where the majority of us have looked for happiness.

When we start focusing on the nature of happiness itself, rather than what appears to point to happiness, we experience true happiness and freedom. We must first concentrate on the nature of who we are before concentrating on the nature of happiness. All that we may want is made known to us as we embark on the never-ending journey into the self.

This book teaches you how to change your perception. You can take part in the unending journey into the self by changing your perspective from the world of objects to the nature of consciousness. This book is structured into five chapters, each of which focuses on a distinct metaphysical core idea to aid you in your journey. Each chapter, in turn, represents a week of simple daily routines that you might use. By the time this book is finished, you'll have a solid basis for altering the course of your life. Are you prepared to shift your attention from the arrows in your life to the gorgeous moon that represents your truth?

Week 1:

Why Silence Is the Greatest Teacher

The Silent Discovery

Consider yourself entering a forest and coming across a little pond. You fling a tiny rock into the water before peeking inside. The ripples from the splash distort your reflection in its waters. The water surface becomes glass-like smooth and the ripples vanish after a short while. This time, when you gaze into the pond, you perceive both your image as well as that of the surrounding environment, including the trees, mountains, and sky.

For the majority of us, life is like a pond with ripples in it. Because of the distortion we encounter, we are never able to see life or ourselves. The distortion I refer to is the wave of illusions produced when our understanding of our true nature is clouded.

Because we have lost the stillness within us, which was our direct link to the essence of who we are, we have clarity regarding our true nature. The good news is that the silence I refer to has never been lost and cannot be. Instead, because we were obsessed with the stuff, we have forgotten about it.

Because we have been indoctrinated to view life as something outside of ourselves, we have forgotten what silence is like. This socialization has been practiced for countless generations. We are preoccupied with the things in our lives because we have cut ourselves off from our true selves. Our sense of ourselves and the caliber of our lives have been defined by these things.

Objects and stillness are natural parts of life. Silence itself is an object. This issue will be covered later in the book. We'll talk about the importance of silence for now. Any sounds that may be present in your area have nothing to do with the silence that we will be exploring. The quiet you feel inside is the silence I'm referring to.

Day 1

Difficult Perception

We'll begin with a little exercise that might help people experience stillness and the nature of awareness (please note that it might take some practice before you get the benefits of this exercise).

1. Take a seat and become comfy.
2. Focus your attention on an item in your surroundings. I want you to focus your attention on this object and observe it.
3. What would you tell me if I asked you to give me a report on what you know about the object?

I would assume that you would provide me with the object's name, a description of how it appears, and possibly a description of what it was doing. For instance, if I were looking at a tree, I could describe its appearance, color, height, and shape of its leaves to you. I might even be able to identify the tree's species and the region in which it is found.

After I've given you an example, look at your object once more. What specific details about your thing do you know?

You have completed this exercise, and we are now ready to resume our conversation quiet. If you are like the majority of people, you would provide information and thoughts regarding your subject in your report to me. You might be able to summarize your report to me in a single sentence, or you might be able to go into great detail about your experience.

You will probably think the results of your observation are a true portrayal of your object, regardless of what you report back.

We will now dissect the previous activity to test your ability to observe.

1. Take another look at your object. How do you know the dimensions of your thing, its color, or any other details you observe?

You would probably respond, "Because I saw it," most certainly.

2. Examine your item once more.

Check to see whether you can distinguish between seeing the object and the object itself. Can I distinguish between how I view the tree and the actual tree, in other words? Or, to put it another way, do the process of looking and the thing you are seeing merge into one another at some point? I hope you will understand the close connection between the act of seeing and the thing being seen.

3. Assuming you concur with me that your object must exist to be seen, I have the following question for you: How do you know when seeing is occurring?
4. You are aware of it, so you are aware that the act of seeing is occurring. You are aware that seeing is happening.

5. Recheck your object one more. Can you distinguish between the act of looking and the knowledge of seeing? Take your time to decide whether or not this question is more challenging than the last one. You will eventually come to understand that seeing and being conscious of seeing are the same.

Let's sum up everything we've just learned:

The object itself and the act of seeing it are the same.

The act of seeing itself and the consciousness of the act of looking is both the same.

These insights lead us to the conclusion that nothing exists apart from awareness and that knowledge and knowledge itself are inseparable. Look at your object once more from this fresh angle if you were able to experience what I was directing you toward in this exercise. Do you have a different reaction to what you saw? Changes what you can tell me about your object as a result?

Your first perception of the object was similar to a pond that had just had a boulder thrown into it before you performed this exercise. Your thoughts warped any deeper understanding of your object, similar to how pond ripples affect experiences.

The waves that are produced by your mind's activities will gradually lessen as you perform this exercise using the advice I provided. Your experience of life will be clearer and more united, just like the motionless water of a pond. Applying the preceding experiment to the remaining four senses is also possible.

The ability to remain unaffected by the buzz of our minds and recognize the intricacies of reality that reveal its true nature is silence, also known as stillness. You can only have a knowing (knowledge) of the presence of experience; you cannot know anything about that which you experience.

I do not know trees. I only have my perceptions of the tree to go on. I can hear the sounds of the tree's leaves rustling in the breeze and I can feel the sensations when I touch it. I can understand my thoughts about the tree, but I am unable to comprehend the tree itself. The secrets of the universe will come into view as easily as calm water reflections when awareness illuminates reality without being warped by human thinking.

This is how quiet has power.

Regular exercise

Normally, you need to practice the exercise you completed in this part before you notice a significant shift in how you view the world. Practice this drill once more.

A servant formerly had a master who resided in a substantial mansion.

The relationship between the servant and his master was peculiar because the servant had never met him. The master never left his chamber, and all interactions took place through the bedroom's locked door. The servant would be called to the master's closed door to receive orders if the master required something.

The servant was once venting to a buddy about his frustration with his master at the time. He revealed to his pal that his master was never content with him and was constantly finding something wrong. His lord was constantly expecting more of him. His friend advised him to talk to his boss about his worries. He found his friend's counsel to be sound. He had to express his feelings to his lord. He mustered up the confidence to approach his master's room and knock on the door. He was surprised when his master did not comment. He knocked again but received no response. The steward became anxious. Was his boss in peril, was that possible?

The janitor mustered up the courage to grab the doorknob. He was shocked to find the door unlocked. He was speechless when he unlocked the door. The space was deserted! There was nothing in the room—no master, no furniture, no carpet, no drapes. The janitor became hopeless. He understood that he had lived his entire life in service to an imaginary master.

The relationship most of us have with our minds is reflected in the narrative you just read. You and I are the servants, and our ideas are the master. Most of us live our lives following our minds, much like servants. Our thoughts continuously demand things from us and never feel fulfilled, just like the master.

Our unwavering commitment to our thoughts is the cause of every issue we face, both individually and collectively.

I'm hoping that by using the fundamental metaphysical ideas in this book, you'll gradually notice a change in how you interact with your mind. You will take control of your thoughts rather than letting them rule you. Your mind will be a tool for us to solve issues, create new possibilities, and explore greater levels of consciousness rather than a dictator that is constantly demanding more of you.

You engaged in tasks in the previous section that encouraged you to consider the nuances of object observation. At the conceptual level, the mind functions. In other words, only those objects that can be perceived by the senses or conceptualized by the mind can be detected by the mind. In our experience, we refer to things that have these characteristics as phenomenal. The mind records everything that can be registered by our senses.

The way the mind works is by conceptually representing the data it gathers from our senses. When I stare at a tree, my eyes gather visual data about the tree, which the optic nerve then converts into electric impulses. The brain decodes the digitized information and reassembles it into a conceptual representation of the tree when the electric impulses reach it.

When we experience anything conceptually, we don't see it as it is; instead, we see an image that the mind has conjured up. The "tree" in my backyard is not the actual thing.

The "tree" that I perceive is a mental construct that I take to be the real tree. This is why I said in the previous part that we can only learn from experience and that we can never know anything about our experiences. The only thing I can know about a tree is its conceptual representation.

Regarding the exercises in the previous section, if you were able to realize that an object's awareness and the object itself are the same, you made a profound realization that most people lack. The fact that the majority of people on earth have not experienced this experience helps us to understand why actual freedom is still for the most part just an abstract concept.

True freedom can only be attained regardless of the circumstances of our lives. More freedom is granted to some prisoners than to some multimillionaires. Real freedom can only be felt once we have mastered our relationship with our minds.

There is not a single issue a person may go through that is not brought on by a constrained sense of self. All acts or behaviors have their roots in thought at their most fundamental level. We start everything we do with a thought. There are just two types of thoughts: scared and loving. Fearful thoughts stem from the belief that we are cut off from the rest of life.

Love-related thoughts come from a sense of unity with life and a connection to others. Sincere, lovable ideas eliminate our sensation of alienation and banish fear. Since most of us experience life through the conceptions we construct for it, it might be difficult for us to feel separate from it.

Imagine visiting the Grand Canyon and finding the most breathtaking natural perspective of the canyon's grandeur. You can see its raging torrents, incredible rock formations, and gorgeously rough canyon walls. You decide to use an inexpensive disposable camera to capture a picture of what you see since you are so fascinated by it.

You notice that the created image in no way resembles what you experienced when you look at it.

Similar to how the image is like our concepts. They are a poor substitute for life's boundless majesty.

Most of us view life via our preconceived notions. Our idea of self is a concept as well. The majority of us are slaves to our minds because we have faith in the ideas that they generate, including our sense of self.

Here is a quick workout. In response to this query: So who are you?

When posed this question, the majority of people respond (if they can respond at all) with statements like I am a male.

- I am a female.

- I'm not deserving.

- I'm a decent person.

- I'm timid.

- I'm a dissident.

- I have kids.

- I am an educator.

- I am successful.

- I am an individual.

- I live in this world as a citizen.

Whatever way you choose to respond to this query, you are defining who you are in terms of concepts. Concepts have become personal to us because we have personalized our experiences with them. Depending on what our minds tell us, we perceive ourselves. We can only transcend conceptions via stillness and come to know for ourselves that part of ourselves that is more fundamental than anything the intellect can comprehend.

Transcending our minds involves altering our interaction with them. We resemble the servant who discovered that his master's room was vacant when we exceed our mental limitations.

Recognizing Reality's Illusions

We have studied the nature of the mind and inner silence thus far in this chapter. We also talked about how we concentrate on the things that make up the magnificent world. Everything that can be perceived by our thoughts or senses is included in the phenomenal world, as we already stated.

The majority of us experience life from an amazing perspective. In other words, the realm of form is the extent of our awareness.

We have grown to identify with the world of form because that is where we concentrate our attention. The phenomenal frequently shapes how we perceive ourselves and how we define ourselves. Here is an illustration: Joe is on his way to work in his automobile when a distracted driver cuts him off. Joe becomes enraged and swears at the other driver. Joe's supervisor informs him that he will receive a bonus when he reports to work. Joe is pleased to learn this information.

Later on that day, Joe receives a call from a challenging customer. Joe gets irritated. Joe returns home at the end of the day to the hug of his loved ones. Joe now feels cherished and encouraged.

Joe went through a variety of emotional states throughout the day, and each feeling altered how Joe felt about himself. He also thought that the scenarios he encountered were to blame for the fluctuations in his mental condition. He blames the other driver, the bonus, the challenging customer, and his family for these developments. Joe is an illustration of how the circumstances and events in our lives impact how we feel about ourselves.

Our concept of self is fragile since change is an inevitable part of existence. We can experience fleeting feelings of being on top of the world before feeling defeated when the winds of change pass us by.

Now, think about your own life. What aspects of your life have altered since you were a little child? Have your ideas evolved? Have your opinions evolved? Your relationships—have they changed? Has your body altered? Has the way you perceive the world changed? Has your perspective of yourself changed? Everything you have ever known has undergone some sort of transformation. Everything in life is constantly changing, at least on a fantastic scale.

It is not sufficient for us to merely state that everything in life changes.

How can you tell when something is changing? Similar to how you knew about the object in the prior exercise, you are aware that change is taking place. Because you are conscious of it, you are aware of the change.

You must first be conscious of what doesn't change to be aware of the change. If you don't know the contrary, how can you possibly know anything? Without knowledge of hot, how can one understand cold? If you don't also know fury, how can you know calm?

You have a part of yourself that is aware of the change, including the changes you go through cognitively, emotionally, and physically. Because it is changeless, this component of you is aware of the change. The only thing that can perceive change is that which is changeless. How else would change be detectable? There is a part of you that is unfathomable and resides in the silence of your being. The aspect I'm referring to cannot be understood by the intellect because it is non-phenomenal. If something cannot be perceived by the senses or imagined by the mind, it is said to be non-phenomenal.

The unfolding of existence, which is what we refer to as "reality," is something that your non-phenomenal self observes. There is no real reality; rather, what we perceive as reality is a projection of consciousness that is ever-changing.

The delusion of reality is the idea that we exist independently in a physical universe. We perceive ourselves as being distinct from other people, other things, and our surroundings. We strive after things in the physical world in the hope that they will bring us happiness and release us from our pain because we perceive ourselves to be distinct.

We feel a sense of loss or disappointment when things change because nothing in the phenomenal world is eternal.

We run around on a wheel like a hamster. No matter how quickly we run, we can never reach the destination we seek—the location of unbroken serenity. We have bought into the delusion that there is something out there waiting to provide us with the experiences we desire.

The key to achieving ultimate calm is to root ourselves in the constant while relishing the experience of change. Your true self is unchanging. The various manifestations of your core nature are what change. The shape that your essential being uses to experience its many manifestations is what you perceive to be who you are. It was previously mentioned that experience itself and knowledge of experience are inseparable. Your awareness is who you are at your core, and experience is all you are aware of.

You are one with everything because awareness and experience are inseparable.

Regular exercise

This exercise can help you become more adept at perceiving without understanding what you are experiencing:

1. Take a seat and observe your surroundings, slowing down to fully take them in.
2. When you're prepared, close your eyes and permit yourself to unwind.
3. Assume you are an extraterrestrial visiting Earth to learn more about it. You don't know anything about this planet, and you don't have any previous experiences to depend on.
4. As a result, you are unable to categorize, pinpoint, evaluate, or pass judgment on whatever you encounter. You are therefore a clean slate.
5. Do not open your eyes and take another glance around you. Give it some time.
6. How did your second observational experience differ from the first?

If there was no difference between the two observations that you made, repeat the exercise until there is. When we observe something while including our opinions or judgments, we conceptualize what we are seeing. Being aware and present includes being able to perceive without using conceptual thinking.

Day 4:

Exceptional vs. Non-Exceptional

The terms phenomenal and non-phenomenal have been used frequently in this chapter. In a nutshell, phenomenal refers to whatever you can experience. Our current understanding of the planet is astounding. Non-phenomenal is anything that exists but cannot be perceived by us. Our minds operate conceptually, which means that any piece of information that enters them is transformed into a notion.

Examples of mental constructions that are conceptual are words and images. Only the human mind can produce words and images. Words and images would not exist without the mind. Images are not what we "see." As previously said, visual information is taken in by our eyes and translated into electrical impulses. The brain subsequently transforms the electrical impulses into visuals. Similar to how sentences are linguistic creations of the mind, words are also employed to express ideas. You might be wondering why I use "brain" instead of "mind."

I'm writing this way for the time being just for semantics' sake. The distinction between the mind and the brain will be covered later.

If words are the mind's representation of thought and visuals are the results of the information gathered by sight, where do information and thought originate? Information and thought are the same. We refer to the information that consciousness perceives as thought. Everything that exists is, at its core, information. We may, however, go a step further.

Energy is a type of information. Energy manifests itself in all that is. But this energy is not the same as the energy we encounter every day. I'm not referring to electrical energy here. The energy I'm referring to is conscious of itself. I'm talking about the energy of consciousness.

You completed an exercise in which you had to observe an object in the first chapter of this book. Hopefully, after completing this task, you concluded that it is impossible to distinguish between an object's awareness and its actual form. The phrases "awareness" and "consciousness" simply refer to the same concept. Everything that exists has consciousness at its core. The origin of everything is consciousness.

There can be no experience if there is no consciousness.

Returning to the categories non-phenomenal and phenomenal, these are merely explanations provided by our mind for what it is capable of perceiving and what it is not. Words, ideas, the mind, this book, and you are just the outward expressions of consciousness. The phenomenal realm and a non-phenomenal realm are identical at their most fundamental levels. Between materialism and spirituality, there is no distinction. The lines between fantasy and reality are blurred. Finally, there is no distinction between the universe and you. Any perception of differentiation or difference is a creation of the mind.

Some scientists devote countless hours to studying the universe's beginnings or the makeup of matter. There will be no end to their searches. When the solutions they seek are hidden in the depths of their own lives, they are chasing concepts instead.

Regular exercise

1. Get comfortable and start to unwind.
2. take a second to examine a familiar object. Focus your attention on this item only.
3. Once you are comfortable with the thing, close your eyes and use your best mental imagery to create a mental picture of it.
4. Do not criticize your capacity to visualize because everyone visualizes differently. To the best of your ability, visualize your object.
5. Once the image is in your head, take note of its characteristics. What do you make of this picture? Is it clear or blurry? Has it brilliant detail or is it faint without any recognizable features? Do the characteristics of your image fluctuate in strength or shape, or do they remain constant?
6. Can you pinpoint the origin of your image and the direction it travels after it fades?
7. Now picture an imaginary, unreal object that does not exist in your world. It might be an elephant with purple fur or a unicorn.
8. Once the image is in your head, take note of its characteristics. What do you make of this picture? Is it clear or blurry? Has it brilliant detail or is it faint without any recognizable features? Do the characteristics of

your image fluctuate in strength or shape, or do they remain constant?

9. Can you identify the source of your image? When your image fades, can you tell where it goes?

Is there a difference between the fictional item you visualized and the one you observed? Do you have the ability to distinguish between "reality" and "fantasy"?

Five-day

meditation

This first chapter has so far covered topics such as silence, mental deceptions, phenomenal and non-phenomenal existence, and quiet.

Though everything you have read up to this point is merely an idea, I hope you have found this conversation to be fascinating. It has merely served as fodder for thought. Concepts are an essential component of human existence. We need concepts to exchange ideas because we are social creatures. Concepts are crucial in this regard.

The mind operates in the same way. Our ability to evolve successfully depends on our minds. Our capacity for problem-solving is what has contributed most to our species' domination. Our species' tragedy is that we have become mentally identified. We think that our intellect and body define who we are.

We behave out of fear due to our sense of separation—which is brought on by our identification with our mind and body—fear of loss and fear of scarcity. All of our problems, whether they are personal or societal, start from this perspective. Additionally, it restricts our ability to reach higher states of consciousness and awareness.

Consider a playwright who is acting in it. This actor is faultless in how she portrays her character to the audience and has a strong emotional connection to it. She takes off her makeup, changes her clothes, and leaves for home after the play. Her character is no longer portrayed by the actor. She is now transitioning into a wife, mom, friend, or daughter. She might go out on a date, go camping, or party with her buddies. What the performer can do off stage is endless.

When we identify with the mind or body, we are similar to the actor who, after the play is finished, continues to think she is her character. To encounter the deeper and more fundamental aspects of who we are, we must learn to transcend our brains. Meditation is one of the most effective strategies for this. In meditation, stillness is the central focus. It detects the false appearances of reality and establishes a link between ourselves and the non-phenomenal world.

Regular exercise

When learning meditation techniques, it's important to bear the following in mind:

1. Keep an attitude of absolute acceptance and uncriticism toward all you go through.
2. Refrain from attempting to alter, change, or resist everything you encounter.
3. Give everything you encounter the freedom to fully express itself.
4. You can have thoughts like:
5. My thoughts keep arriving; they are not slowing down when you are meditating.
6. This is too challenging.

7. This is monotonous.
8. I have more pressing matters to attend to.
9. This is ineffective.

Am I performing this correctly?

Ignore them and keep your attention on the meditation.

Finally, as long as you are allowing yourself to be a witness to all of your experiences, there is no right or wrong method to meditate.

1. Take a seat comfortably, close your eyes, and take a deep breath.
2. Direct your attention to the feelings of your breath entering and leaving your body.
3. As you keep your attention on your breathing, thoughts will start to surface. Simply ignore them when they appear and focus once more on your breathing.
4. If you maintain your attention on your breath, a time will eventually come when you can do so effortlessly.
5. When you get to this point, permit yourself to just watch everything that comes into your awareness.
6. Pay attention to how ideas, feelings, and impressions flash into your awareness before disappearing. In your awareness, these mental entities appear and vanish. That which is awareness, however, does not change and remains constant.
7. The mental events you encounter may be pleasant, neutral, or negative, but awareness itself is unaffected by any of these characteristics.
8. As you give mental occurrences less priority, they will lose some of their intensity and your mind will become

calmer. You might even go through moments of stillness and space. If you do, be aware that space and quiet are also mental phenomena. Remain a witness to your experiences rather than attaching yourself to them.

9. Keep meditating for however long you like.

Day 6

What Kind of Experience It Is

We see ourselves to be a distinct and independent entity that exists in a world of other entities, both living and non-living since we identify with our thoughts and bodies. The words that appear on the screen of my laptop as I sit here and compose this piece are visible to me. In addition, I am aware of the room I am in, my wife's whereabouts upstairs, and the presence of my dog on the carpet. I am conscious of both myself and the tune that is playing on the radio.

I think the words, the room I'm in, my wife, my dog, and the song are separate things that exist outside of myself because I have ideas and physical experiences. These other things collectively are what people typically refer to as "experience."

It is impossible to separate the awareness of an experience from the experience itself, as we discussed in this chapter's first section.

For you to experience what I'm talking about firsthand, I'll give you another practice. When investigating the metaphysical, direct experience is essential. We are left with nothing but a theory in the absence of firsthand experience.

Regular exercise

The following activity will challenge you further to consider how you perceive reality, building on the first exercise from the previous day.

1. Find a comfortable seat, close your eyes, and give yourself some time to unwind.
2. While taking a normal breath, concentrate on the direction of the breath.
3. Take note of the feelings you have as your breath enters and exits your body.
4. If your thoughts should divert your attention, just bring it back to your breathing.
5. As you concentrate on your breath, refrain from passing judgment on whatever experiences you have. Without attempting to alter or adjust it, accept every experience you have.
6. Let go of whatever expectations you may have while you concentrate on your breathing. Make no effort at all. Allow all that occurs to take place.
7. When you are peaceful and at ease, switch your attention from your breath to your thoughts.
8. Take note of your awareness of your ideas. What happens to your thoughts when you maintain mental focus? Does anything alter the way you think? Do they fluctuate in intensity?

Do they appear and then disappear over time? What inspires your thoughts? When they disappear, where do they go?

9. At this point, focus your attention on your body's feelings rather than your thoughts.

10. Recognize that you are conscious of your feelings. What happens to your sensations while you keep your attention on them? Your feelings do alter in any way? Do they fluctuate in intensity? Do they appear and then disappear over time? What causes your feelings to occur? When they disappear, where do they go?

11. Reach out and touch something while keeping your eyes closed. Your arm or leg, the item you're sitting on, anything in the room, or even you could be the culprit.

12. When you touch something, consider if you are experiencing the item itself or the object's experience. Can you distinguish the object's sensation from the actual object? From where does this feeling come?

When this feeling vanishes, where does it go? You should decide the answers to these questions.

13. Recognize that you are conscious of how a sensation changes as it arrives and disappears.

14. Check to see if you can distinguish between the sensation itself and your awareness of it.

15. 14. At this point, open your eyes and look at something. Ask yourself whether you can distinguish between seeing the thing and seeing itself as you pay attention to it. You must decide the response to this question.

16. Consider whether you can distinguish between the consciousness of seeing and the actual seeing.
17. Once more, shut your eyes and take a moment to unwind.

When you're at ease, consider whether it's possible to have experiences without being aware of them. You must decide the response to this question.

18. Consider whether it's possible to distinguish between the knowledge of experience and the experience itself.

I'm hoping you'll see that experience and consciousness are the same. This is true because awareness, also known as consciousness, is the source of experience. The phenomenal manifestation of awareness, which is non-phenomenal, is what we refer to as experience. When you realize this, you'll intuitively understand that any sense of separation is an illusion produced by the conceptual mind. Everything is one from higher levels of consciousness.

You were unable to pinpoint the location of where ideas and sensations appear and disappear since they do so within consciousness. The things you touched or observed were also created by consciousness. Even the awareness that you are alive and existing is an indication of consciousness. Consciousness is the source of your awareness. It is from the consciousness that you derive who you think you are.

You perceive a physical body because it enables you to experience the phenomenal world. This is why you believe you have a physical body. The essential element of the universe is energy, and energy that is aware, as was explained earlier in this book. That energy is consciousness, and consciousness is continuously growing as we learn more. Information can only is obtained via experience.

Consciousness can only experience itself since it lacks phenomenality. In other words, only awareness itself can know itself. It must manifest as phenomenal objects, like you and I, to have an experience and gather information. Experience is the main source of learning.

Every time you have an experience, you are passing along the knowledge you learned from it to the pure consciousness (from which you originally manifested). We think about the knowledge we learn through experience.

Consciousness receives knowledge from the thought that it can use to expand and produce new manifestations that are congruent with the information. This process, which the pure mind does continuously, is what is usually referred to as the Law of Attraction.

Day 7

Psychology of the Self

We see the world at a conceptual level, therefore it can be challenging to understand that we are phenomenal representations of bigger consciousness. For this concept to be self-evident, our typical consciousness awareness must be transcended. Fortunately, most of us achieve this transcendence at night when we go to sleep.

You enter a different state of consciousness when you dream at night. You feel in the dream as your dream self as it progresses. Your dream self experiences the dream world it is in and thinks, feels, and perceives it. As it interacts with its dream world, it can decide, plan, anticipate, and take action. Even while your dream may appear to be real while it is happening, it is a projection of your sleeping self. Similar to this, your perception of yourself as a distinct and individual being while you are awake is also a projection of pure consciousness.

It becomes clear to us when we wake up from a dream that the dream self we encountered was only a psychological representation of ourselves. Because consciousness is associated with it, our dream persona and its dream experience seemed incredibly real to us. Our dream was built on relevant notions for us, which is why consciousness is connected with it. In a similar vein, you identify with your body and mind because the ideas and convictions you have about them have personal significance for you.

Similar to how your waking self is the psychological self that is a projection of pure awareness, your dream self is a psychological self that you experience when you're asleep. There is a level of consciousness where we can transcend our psychological selves, though.

We are not thinking during deep sleep, unlike dream sleep. Pure awareness exists during deep sleep. Pure consciousness turns its awareness away from the realm of things (which includes thoughts) as we fall asleep and toward itself. Deep slumber is a state of awareness watching awareness.

We don't remember deep slumber because it is thoughtless at that time.

Deep sleep lacks experience, which is necessary for memory formation. We are aware that we had a deep sleep when we wake up in the morning, but we are not aware of the experience itself. Additionally, when we fall asleep deeply, we become completely unconscious. We had forgotten our existence as individuals, which is why we awoke from deep slumber feeling refreshed and alive. Because our fundamental selves were reconnected, we lost sight of who we were as individuals.

Regular exercise

The following activity emphasizes self-reflection as you examine the characteristics of the entity that you identify as "you." You mustn't rely on what you think you know when carrying out this exercise.

Instead, I want to base this exercise solely on your personal experiences. Follow your experience rather than your thoughts. I also advise you to read this meditation thoroughly before beginning it. Alternately, record it on audio tape and listen to it while performing this exercise.

1. Don't rely on your thinking to come up with an answer to this question. You won't receive a response.
2. Take a seat comfortably and close your eyes.
3. Permit yourself to observe the inhalation and exhalation of your breath. Concentrate on your breathing. As it flows through your body, feel it.
4. Adopt a mindset of complete allowing, in which you accept everything that occurs during this meditation.
5. Pay attention to your internal observations, thoughts, feelings, and emotions. Allow them to arrive and depart of their own volition. All you have to do is watch them from a distance.
6. You are the one who is watching what you think, feel, perceive, and feel. The only person who is aware of experience is you. Who are you though? You use the pronoun "I" to refer to yourself, but who am I?
7. Where am I, exactly? Can you pinpoint the location of this "I"? Does it exist within you? Is it in the center of your chest?
8. The term "phenomenal" refers to something that can be perceived through sight, thought, touch, sound, or other senses. 9. Recognize that everything you come across is magnificent as you look for the place of "I."

9. Everything you know and everything you encounter is fantastic.

10. You are not space, nothingness, or happiness, notwithstanding any experiences to the contrary. Space, emptiness, and bliss are phenomenal as well because you can sense them.

11. Are you amazing? Everything wonderful is a work in progress. Your thoughts, feelings, and emotions are ever-changing experiences.

12. Your thoughts enter and exit your awareness

13. Who is watching thought enter and exit awareness? Are you waking up and falling asleep?

14. Do Your sentiments and emotions fluctuate all the time?

15. Are you always evolving?

16. Your response, regardless of how you answer these questions, is aware. What knows you responded?

17. Your true self is eternal and does not change.

18. Your identity is not something that can be seen, felt, or detected. Your identity is not extraordinary.

19. You cannot experience who you are. The very awareness of who you are. The awareness that is you cannot observe itself, just as a lightbulb cannot shine on itself. You are aware of your existence.

20. You'll get closer to understanding who you are as you learn more about what you're not.

21. This concludes the meditation. Permit yourself to keep quiet for as long as you choose.

Week 2

How the Mind Creates Reality: The Power of Thoughts and Beliefs

If we compare ideas to bits for a computer, then we may say that thought are informational units.

We believe that we are the creators of thought and that the thoughts we have to belong to us since we identify with our minds and bodies. Your psychological self appears to be thinking at the same time that your dream self appears to be thinking.

All things are one at their most basic level. Our manifested selves attract thoughts that are congruent with the level of consciousness we have attained, which is what we mistakenly perceive as "our thoughts." Every living thing can access the collective consciousness and draw information that is in line with its conscious awareness. The collective consciousness, also known as the Akashi Records, is the repository of all past, present, and future thoughts.

All facets of awareness are included in the broader consciousness system. It encompasses all expressions of consciousness, including pure awareness, as well as the localized consciousness that each expressed form of consciousness experiences.

Pure consciousness naturally seeks expansion and works to make each of its manifestations successful and happy. These actions are performed by pure consciousness via thought.

The information that is produced by experience and fed into the larger consciousness system is thought. Additionally, the expansion of consciousness—both of pure consciousness and that of its localized expressions—comes through the enlightening of the many elements of the broader consciousness system.

A little youngster (a manifestation of awareness that has localized consciousness) is attempting to solve a mathematical puzzle.

The problem is not resolved as a result of the child's efforts. The concept that the child is attracted to is what drives his or her efforts.

A sense of contrast is felt when thoughts result in actions that do not achieve the expected result. In this instance, the difference arises from the fact that despite the child's experiences, the intended outcome (the solution to the problem) did not materialize.

The experience of contrast increases consciousness, which encourages the manifestation of additional phenomena that are consistent with the child's desired result. As a result, the youngster has access to ideas for resolving the issue that they had not previously considered. The child tries several approaches to the issue until it is resolved. Localized consciousness (that of the child) and pure consciousness both grow as a result of the flow of information (thought).

The mental image of awareness' limitless expressive potential is thought. The thoughts that we attract are like a snapshot of that infinite intelligence because our conceptual mind prevents us from experiencing the infinite potential of consciousness. Comparing a single frame to the entire movie it came from will help you comprehend this better. The majority of us are only conscious enough to detect one frame at a time. The more of the movie we can experience, the greater level of conscious consciousness we reach.

Applying the lessons from metaphysics to our daily lives can help us become more conscious, which is the ultimate goal of studying it. We get closer to recognizing the truth of our existence the more our awareness expands.

Thoughts are informational snippets, whereas beliefs are the thoughts we accept as true. Beliefs are those ideas for which we have a strong sense of assurance. In keeping with the movie metaphor, clinging to a belief is comparable to us viewing a single frame of a movie and concluding that we are aware of its plot.

Our experience of life is influenced by our beliefs because we feel confident in them. Beliefs alter how we perceive the world and ourselves, much like a pair of tinted sunglasses. My perception of the world will be based on whether I think it's dangerous or not. My experience of life will reflect my belief that love is the basis of existence.

Thoughts come from the non-phenomenal, just like everything else that is phenomenal. Additionally, ideas play a crucial role in the manifestation process. The first step in the manifestation process is the manifestation of desire. The first and most basic manifestation of unadulterated consciousness is desire. When the knowledge that is consistent with want is present in thinking, desire then manifests as thought. Emotions are the result of thought. The action takes the physical form of emotions and vice versa. We are so accustomed to this procedure that we are not even conscious of it.

Additionally, we just focus on the last stage, which is the actual manifestation. The majority of us are oblivious to every step that comes before the manifestation. Additionally, we accept responsibility or blame for the outcome.

Consider a situation where a person is struggling to make ends meet and needs to boost their income. The urge to make more money is the manifestation of a solution to this person's problem. As a result of desire, one begins to think about what one can do to improve their circumstances. The thoughts that a person attracts can include thoughts about seeking a new career, the kind of job they want, ideas for better money management, and so on.

This person attracts thoughts that eventually manifest as emotions.

Emotion provides the drive to put ideas into action. This person's emotions may include worry, irritation, or desire for changing their fiancé. They may also include fear or passion for their existing circumstances. Emotions are the catalyst for transformation in either case. Passion propels them onward as they are motivated to change by the pain of financial hardship.

Then, emotion turns into action: The individual looks for career openings distributes resumes, and creates a spending plan. As long as you remain focused, your actions will eventually take on tangible forms, such as more money and a new career.

You'll see that we place all of our attention on the action component as a result of our socialization process, which makes us identify with our mind and body. All the earlier processes led to the actual manifestation, the new job, and the increased income. The final step, the action step, is what turned on the innate power present in each of the preceding processes.

Day 8

Morals

This week, you should focus on changing your thoughts and beliefs to make them more supportive of you by lowering the resistance you feel inside. You can increase your alignment with pure consciousness by lowering your resistance. Locating your values is the focus of day eight.

Values serve as a barometer for our priorities in life. Contrary to how values are typically understood, the values I refer to have to do with the emotional or mental states that we cherish. A typical traditional value would be family, for instance. Family is not a value in the context of our discussion.

The emotional states that a family gives us are valuable, nevertheless. Values include, for instance:

- Love

- Compassion Contribution Security

- Fun

- Transcendence

We face significant resistance in our lives whenever we act in a way that is at odds with our ideals. Start the process of making changes in your life if your lifestyle does not currently reflect your values to begin achieving greater harmony. What can you do to make the necessary changes in your work if your current position is at odds with your values? Could your work be done differently?

Would you have to take on a different role? It can entail looking for a new position. What adjustments must you do if the relationship you are in does not reflect your values? Should you change your current relationship or look for a new one? Consider any area of your life where there is a discrepancy between your actions and the principles you uphold.

Examples of causing resistance by acting against our values include the following:

You cherish enthusiasm, yet you don't pursue your aspirations because you're afraid of losing the stability of your hated employment.

You cherish relationships, but you spend all of your time working rather than with your family. You appreciate personal development but consistently follow the same path simply because you were taught or brought up to think that's how things should be done.

Regular exercise

Make a list of your core beliefs and rank them in order of importance. What is most important in my life? is a question you can use to determine your values. Remember, you are going for states of emotion or feeling. If your family or your finances are your top priorities, think about the emotions or sentiments that each might bring you.

Check to see whether how you live your life contradicts each value you've identified.

Here's an illustration:

1. What is the most significant thing in my life? my spouse

2. The emotional emotions I cherish make up my values. My wife provides me with love and connection, therefore they are the things I truly appreciate.

3. I must examine my life to see if any aspects go against my desire for love and kinship. Example: When she gets angry with me, I become defensive.

Day 9

beliefs

You determined your values on Day 8. You will determine today which of your key beliefs can be at odds with what you value.

The competing beliefs we hold are ultimately to blame for the opposition we encounter in life. Often, simply recognizing the thought that is causing resistance will cause that belief to lose some of its power. The practice that comes next is for figuring out the beliefs that are causing your reluctance.

Regular exercise

Make a note of the circumstances in your life that are upsetting or frustrating you. Expand on the items you write for your list so that you are aware of everything that is involved. Example: Write "When my spouse criticizes me" in place of "When I lost my spouse." This list will be utilized in the day-ten exercise.

Day 10

Getting to know your values

After you've finished making your list, decide which item is most crucial for you to address. When you've decided on your object, I want you to rewrite it in the following way: "What does it represent to me? I've used the issue "I feel upset because my boss is continuously criticizing me" as an example of how to approach this activity.

1. I change the way I phrase my issue to read: "What does it mean to me when my supervisor criticizes me?"
2. I would then answer that query by writing, "It means that he is unfair," in my response.
3. After that, I would inquire inside, "What does it mean to me that he is unfair?
4. In response, I would reply, "It means he doesn't like me."
5. After that, I would inquire, "What does it imply to me that he doesn't value me?"
6. My response would be, "It indicates I'm not good enough."
7. After that, I would inquire as to what it means that I am insufficient.
8. My response would be, "It says I am not worthwhile."

You want to keep thinking along these lines until you run out of questions to ask.

I think that I am first upset by my boss's comments. The fundamental idea that is bothering me, though, is that I don't think I'm valuable. I react negatively to my boss' behavior because I am unaware it is my core belief. If I had a sincere sense of value, I would look for solutions to problems that would help both my boss and me.

Day 11

Change a Belief

You will transform the belief you recognized on Day 10 in this part.

overcoming restrictive beliefs

You can alter your root belief by using the exercise below once you have determined it (from the previous exercise):

1. Obtain two pieces of paper. Choose 8" x 11" or greater print sizes.
2. Fold the initial piece of paper in half lengthwise.
3. List your core concept at the top of the page.
4. List all the ways this idea has cost you in your life on the left-hand side of the paper. Consider how this root thought has affected you in every area of your life as you do this portion of the exercise. Inquire about the impact this idea has had on your self-perception, relationships, work, finances, physical and mental health, and other aspects of your life.
5. Bear the following in mind when writing:

Write down the first idea that comes to mind when making this list, even if it seems unimportant.

Write as quickly as you can while experiencing the feelings that occur.

This is not a cerebral exercise; it is a passionate exercise.

Write continuously until you run out of topics to cover.

6. For each item you list, give it an arbitrary point number to indicate how much of an impact it has had on you. Choose the first number that pops into your head when deciding on the point value.
7. After all the point values have been assigned, add them all up and put the result at the bottom of the page.
8. Repeat steps 6-7 for the right side of the page, but this time list all the advantages this idea has given you.

When you have finished Step 8, consider a fresh, empowering alternative belief. If my initial thought was, for instance, that "No one will ever love me," then my new belief might be, "The only love I can count on is the love that I offer to myself."

Repeat steps 1 through 8 using your new belief on the second page, with the following modifications: By listing all the ways you think you will profit from your new belief for Step 6, reverse Steps 6 and 8. As you complete Step 8, list all the ways you think it will cost you.

Once you have finished both sheets, proceed as follows:

1. Review your lists right away, allowing yourself to feel any feelings that come up completely.

2. Go over your lists twice a day—once in the morning and once before bed—until you can fully identify with the feelings you are having.

Your mind will be programmed with your new belief once you have properly contrasted the costs of holding onto your old idea with the advantages of embracing your new viewpoint.

Day 12

Getting Ready for Change

You will build a list of actions you can take in this exercise that is consistent with the new, empowering belief you created in the last exercise. Here's an illustration:

I used to hold the core notion that "I am not worthy."

My new conviction (as a result of the exercise on day 11) is that "I am worthy simply by the fact that I exist."

I developed a list of every action I could take to prove my worthiness for today's exercise. For instance:

I'll get myself a nice dinner.

- Respect my emotions and devote the entire day to what I want to do.

- Embark on the journey I've been wanting to take forever.

I want you to choose a time and date once you've finished making your list so that you may commit to taking the actions you've chosen.

Acceptance and resistance on days 13 and 14.

We perceive ourselves as being distinct from the rest of the world because we believe we have a mind and body.

We fight the parts of our existence that hurt, including particular ideas or sensations, because we perceive ourselves as being separate.

If you were in a horrible relationship, you could find it difficult to think about it or feel the emotions and sensations of your unresolved hurt. We cut ourselves off from our inner selves when we fight our thoughts and feelings. By identifying with the thoughts and sensations we are trying to avoid, we break our connection to pure consciousness. We wouldn't reject our unpleasant thoughts and sensations if we didn't identify with them, which would free us up to concentrate on stillness and the nature of consciousness.

The ability to let go of our resistance and our affiliation with the thing we are rejecting is the power of acceptance. As I mentioned before, we draw to our thoughts that are compatible with our sense of who we are. If we are putting our attention on something we don't want, that is what we are doing when we are resisting any aspect of who we are. Without being aware of it, we cannot withstand anything.

We lessen our attachment to our experiences by learning to tolerate them. When I talk about acceptance, I don't mean that we should suppress our emotions and act as though nothing is happening. Instead of resisting the situation, acceptance entails accepting its reality. We may focus on what we want after we accept the current circumstances.

Going against the things we value most in life is one of the ways we build resistance in our lives. When I feel vulnerable but get defensive because I value love and connection, I am resisting what I cherish. You can find situations in your life where your values are at odds by using the task that follows.

Regular exercise

Accepting to do things that go against our true feelings is another way we build resistance within ourselves. This is covered in the following exercise.

You should set out a day to do solely the activities that make you feel wonderful. Since our parents and society have conditioned us to be responsible, many people find this exercise to be challenging. We think that to feel good about ourselves, we must behave responsibly and live up to others' expectations. If you are having problems with this workout, start by doing it for a shorter amount of time and progressively extend the time until you can do it for the entire day.

This activity might seem unrealistic to you. We all have to do some things that we would prefer to avoid. This practice is more concerned with the opposition we are facing than it is with the work at hand. If there is something that needs your attention but you are resisting it, your objective is to lessen that resistance before you start the task.

The actions listed below will help you reduce your resistance.

1. Consider the advantages of completing the assignment and the negative effects of failing to do so. You should have less reluctance to perform the task if the advantages of doing so outweigh the drawbacks.
2. Consider how you could alter the way you approach the duties to make them more pleasurable.

For instance, if you need to remove weeds from your garden, play your favorite music as you work.

3. If none of the aforementioned suggestions make a difference in how you feel about the activity, put it off until you reach a position where you can complete it with acceptance.

The focus for Week Three

Using the Mind as a Sword to Cut Through Obstacles

We have discussed the nature of silence, awareness, experience, and ideas and beliefs throughout the last two chapters. Except for experience, most of us think of these things as mind-related. The purpose of meditation, according to various traditions, is to create a "quiet mind." We also think that the mind is where consciousness, thoughts, and beliefs are stored.

Regarding the mind, many spiritual systems portray it as our adversary and claim that it prevents us from achieving enlightenment.

We have read this book far enough that I feel prepared to dispel another myth that the majority of us have accepted. The mind does not exist. No such thing as a mind. We have established numerous concepts, including that of the mind. You have a psychological self, and the psychological self believes in something called a "mind," too. Your psychological self and your mind are both concepts that our species has come to believe are real.

The strength of beliefs is demonstrated by the fact that the majority of the human population believes they are a physical body with a mind. The belief in the existence of a mind is no different from other beliefs in that it shapes our experience. The attraction of thoughts to our most fundamental notion, the psychological self, is what we take to be the mind.

Our ingrained belief that we possess a mind makes it simpler to work with the mind to transcend it than it is to go up against it.

It will soon become clear that neither our minds nor our psychological selves are genuine as we progress in awareness. We develop the ability to acknowledge them as illusionary qualities without developing emotional attachments to or personifying them. The mind is merely another object in consciousness, which is our true self, just like anything else we perceive.

Even though the mind is an illusion, our thoughts have limitless power. Because it is a consciousness projection that reflects the limitless capacity of consciousness, it has endless power.

We become like servant who unquestionably serves our master when we personalize our thinking by believing that it defines who we are. When you can examine your mind and put some distance between yourself and it, you are heading in the direction of having your mind serve you.

Our capacity to regulate our focus alone determines our capacity to command our brains and advance to higher planes of consciousness. The core of all lessons, whether they are metaphysical or not, is the capacity to manage our focus.

Our capacity to focus our attention is what enables us to increase consciousness, whether it be through math problem-solving or transcending thought. True freedom ultimately results from the shifting of attention away from objects and toward awareness itself. For this work, I consider actual freedom to be the capacity to go beyond the perceived constraints imposed by identification with the mind and body.

You will discover strategies for using your focus to transcend the sense of restriction imposed by our belief in the mind over the remaining days of this week and enhance the quality of your life.

Problem-Solving for Day 15

Once, Albert Einstein said, "No issue can be resolved at the same level of consciousness that brought it into being. Every issue we face is the result of our thinking. Our tendency to think of ourselves as being apart from other people is the mistake in our thinking that causes humanity's issues. Because everything in life is interconnected, when we neglect this fact, we produce issues.

Our failure to see how everything in life is connected extends beyond only our interactions with individuals close to us. It also includes our failure to recognize how we are related to our true selves. We find ourselves being influenced by our constrained views as a result of this ignorance.

Such beliefs include things like "It can't be done."

"That notion is absurd."

I must be realistic and admit that I will never understand this.

"It's too difficult."

"I have tried everything."

"I usually experience this."

"I'm not intelligent enough,"

"I don't know how to do it,"

"I'm giving up,"

As was previously mentioned, the thoughts we have to attract additional thoughts of a like nature. By using intention and silence, one can practice problem-solving from higher states of awareness. To solve a problem from a higher level of awareness, follow these fundamental steps:

Silence: We can achieve a condition of mental tranquility by engaging in meditation, spending time in nature, engaging in physical activity, or by any other method that suits us. You want to enter a peaceful but aware condition, no matter how you get there. The most effective approach to do this is through meditation.

Declare your objective to yourself in a confident manner once you have attained a condition of mental calmness. You must have faith in the viability of your goals. Your doubt will be transmitted to the larger consciousness system if you have any. Here are some examples of intentions:

- I am employed in my ideal position.

- I'm mending my marriage.

- I'm getting more powerful.

- I've overcome this difficulty.

- When the moment is right, I'll find the answer to my issue.

- My issue already has a solution; all I have to do is be open to accepting it.

- I am loving the process of discovering the solution to my problem.

Knowing that I am acquiring the ability to tap into higher levels of awareness for problem-solving makes me feel wonderful.

Keep in mind that not all of these examples aim to get at the solution to the problem. Some of these goals are more process-focused than result-focused. Go with a process-oriented aim if you are unsure that your intention will be realized.

Example:

Result-oriented: I'm mending my marriage.

Process-oriented: I'm having fun discovering more about my marriage.

It makes no difference whether your objectives are process- or results-oriented; both will lead you to the solution when the moment is appropriate for you to get it.

Keep in mind the following standards while you formulate your intentions:

They must be heartfelt.

Your intentions must have a positive impact on everyone who is affected by them.

They must be expressed positively.

The present tense must be used to express them.

Detachment

Detachment exercises are the next step after communicating your desire. Focusing on something unrelated to your problem to become detached. You run the danger of experiencing disappointment or doubt if you keep trying to find the solution to your situation. Your question won't be answered since your dissatisfaction or uncertainty will have a higher frequency than your faith in the manifestation process. The best detachment method is to stop talking, let go of your objective, and get on with your life.

Regular exercise

Make a list of the intentions you have that, if they came true, would mean something to you. Make sure to design them as this section instructs. On Day 16, you'll employ your list.

Day 16

Manifestation on

Use your Day 15 list to practice manifesting for the remainder of this week. Take the actions you learned in Day 15:

1. Go into silence (using meditation is recommended).
2. Tell yourself what you want in private.
3. Work on being detached.

When practicing this exercise, do not get interested in the consequence that you experience.

So, if your intentions do not materialize immediately, try not to be discouraged. Just concentrate on the procedure at first. As you learn to cultivate an attitude of acceptance for whatever happens in your life, your objectives will come to pass.

Day 17 & 18

Visualizations

The subconscious can be accessed and influenced effectively through visualization.

Another effective method for making your intentions a reality is visualization. Some elements of the picturing process, meanwhile, are frequently misunderstood. Consider the following important factors when visualizing:

1. If you have never imagined before, there are many programs available on the market that can be helpful. The best visualizations, nevertheless, are those that you design for yourself. As soon as you comprehend the procedure, just let your imagination go wild.
2. Because they struggle to create distinct mental images, many people believe they are unable to envision. Concerning the quality of your photographs, don't worry. However you experience your visualizations, believe them. Some people just perceive sensations rather than visual representations. Your visualizations will get more vivid with more practice.
3. Setting a purpose for oneself before beginning a visualization exercise is beneficial. Here are some examples of intentions:

    a. Envisioning your desires as already being fulfilled
    b. Imagine yourself investigating the thing you are avoiding.
    c. Imagining yourself tackling a new issue as a type of mental practice.
    d. Visualize yourself resolving a dilemma.

Practice combining the visualization technique into this week's lesson on manifesting your intentions in your daily exercise. Note: Even if you want to keep your intentions separate from yours, you can still see them.

We consider how or when our objectives will come to pass when we are emotionally invested in them. When we picture our goals, we are concentrating on the goal itself, not on how or when it will happen.

Day 19

Changing Attitude

Most of us view the world through the lens of our current situation. A potent tool for developing empathy and understanding with the people in our lives is the capacity to see things from another person's point of view.

1. Consider the individual whose viewpoint you wish to enter.
2. When considering this person, consider their worries and frustrations as well as the causes of those feelings. Your responsibility is to simply acknowledge their complaints; you do not need to comprehend or even concur with their viewpoint.
3. Tell yourself that you want to take on this person's viewpoint.
4. Start your meditation while reaffirming your objective.
5. Restate the aim one final time once you've reached a peaceful mental affirm. Do not attempt to shape your experience or harbor any expectations moving forward. Simply keep an open mind and let whatever arises offer itself to you.
6. Continue doing this exercise until you can see things from the other person's perspective.

7.   This exercise requires practice, just like the majority of the exercises in this book. If you found this exercise ineffective, try not to be dissatisfied. Retraining our minds to respond successfully to this activity takes time. When you're able to make this exercise effective for you, try it out on some animals!

Week 4

We receive feedback from our feelings and emotions on how well we are in alignment with our true selves, which is crucial for the growth of greater levels of awareness. In that we are both phenomenal and non-phenomenal, you and I are both multidimensional beings. Our \sessential self is non-phenomenal whereas our realized form is \sphenomenal. When our phenomenal self and our non-phenomenal self are in harmony, this is what is referred to as "enlightenment."

The thoughts and beliefs we identify with are what push us out of alignment. The alignment procedure is divided into two steps.

Focusing on those ideas that enable and encourage our happiness leads to the first stage of alignment. When we move past all thoughts and concentrate on awareness itself, we have reached the second level. The first stage is the main topic of this section; the second stage was the subject of several of Week 1's tasks.

Emotions are a reflection of our thoughts since they are the tangible embodiment of thought. Our emotions' quality is a reflection of the thoughts we are focusing on at any given time. Because you are concentrating on angry ideas, you are angry. You are concentrating on tranquil ideas, which is why you are experiencing peace. By figuring out which thoughts are making us unhappy, we can strengthen our alignment with pure consciousness.

It can be challenging to pinpoint the thoughts that are making us unhappy, particularly when those thoughts are subconscious. We may easily pinpoint the thoughts that are driving our emotions by focusing on the characteristics of those feelings.

Our emotions reflect our thoughts, but our sensations do not.

They serve as a sign of our union with pure consciousness.

Our emotions are a secondary indicator of alignment, with our feelings serving as the primary indicator. Only our ideas' quality can be determined by our emotions. You should read through these meditations before trying them out, in my opinion. Alternately, record them on audio tape and listen to them while performing this activity.

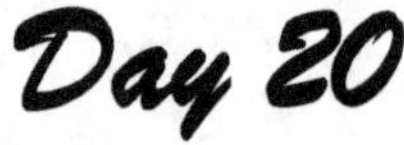

Day 20

of Sensations Observed

We can tell whether we are in sync with our truest selves by how our bodies feel, both pleasurable and unpleasant. You will improve your awareness of your body's sensations by doing this workout.

1. Allow yourself to follow your breath as you inhale and exhale as you close your eyes. Concentrate on your breathing.

    As it flows through your body, feel it.

2. At this point, focus on your body's sensations. Any bodily sensation that comes into your awareness deserves your whole attention.
3. Do the soles of your feet or hands tingle? Do your face, shoulders, or back feel tense? Do the chair or the ground you are sitting on feel heavy to you or do you feel pressure on your buttocks?
4. Permit yourself to feel all of your body's sensations, even the ones that may be unpleasant, without passing judgment on any of them. There is no good or negative experience; sensations are just that—sensations. Value judgments such as good and bad, pleasant and unpleasant, only exist in the mind.

Perceptions, noises, and thoughts all exist just because they do.

5. Are the sensations you feel consistent? Do they ever alter or do they remain the same? Do they linger or do they frequently come and go?
6. Just be conscious of the sensations in your body and give yourself permission to feel them for however long you like.

7. This concludes the meditation; feel free to give yourself
    permission to focus on your body for however long you
    choose.

Day 21

of Emotion Observation

The goal of this meditation is to become aware of your emotions. You can become conscious of your emotions by watching them. By merely being aware of your emotions and learning more about them, you can change them.

1. Take a seat comfortably, then close your eyes.
2. Permit yourself to observe the inhalation and exhalation of your breath. Concentrate on your breathing. As it flows through your body, feel it.
3. Be completely accepting of everything you go through throughout this meditation.
4. Pay attention to your internal observations, thoughts, feelings, and emotions. Allow them to arrive and depart of their own volition. All you have to do is watch them from a distance.
5. Right now, pay attention to any feelings that surface. Become an observer of what occurs when you put your attention on your emotion.
6. Don't assign any significance to the feelings you have or consider them to be either pleasant or negative. Positive, negative, pleasurable, and unpleasant are examples of mental constructs.
7. Nothing in life has an inherent meaning. Every meaning comes from our imaginations. The power we give our emotions and sentiments comes entirely from the attention we give them.

8. When examining emotions, do so with total acceptance; do not make any attempts to change them.

9. Do you notice a change in how you experience your emotions as you pay attention to them? Do they fluctuate in power? Do they get worse or better? Can you pinpoint their origins? Can you track their movements?

10. As you pay attention to your feelings, ask yourself, "Am I experiencing these emotions, or am I the one who is aware of them?" Does awareness feel unpleasant if a feeling or emotion is perceived to be unpleasant? Does awareness feel nice if the emotion is seen as pleasant?

11. Awareness merely clarifies experience; awareness itself is unaffected by the experience. Being aware is like a light beaming on a landscape blanketed in snow. The light merely lights the snow; it doesn't feel the cold of the snow. Be as the light beam while you examine emotions.

12. This concludes the meditation. You are welcome to continue your meditation for as long as you choose.

Day 22

Sensations in Transformation

You may improve your discernment skills and change what you focus on by using mindfulness. You will alter how you perceive feelings by completing this workout.

1. Take a seat and make yourself comfortable. You can choose to close your eyes if you'd like.

2. Focus on the movement of your breath as it enters and exits your body. Allow your body's sensations to come into focus as you let your consciousness flow over it.

3. At this point, search your body with mindfulness for any relaxing, calming, or enjoyable feelings. Allow yourself to concentrate on the sensation when you locate it.

4. I want you to consider the following question as you pay attention to this sensation: "What color is this sensation?" Accept the first answer that pops into your head.

5. Next, inquire as to the magnitude of the sensation. Again, choose the first response that occurs to you.

6. Next, inquire in your mind, "Does this experience have a texture? Is it soft, firm, rough, or smooth?

7. Now look for a bodily experience that is not calm, relaxed, or pleasant. It could have a feeling of pressure, tension, weight, or hardness.

8. Next, ask yourself the same question you asked about the pleasant sensation: "What color, what size, what texture is this sensation?"

9. Allow yourself to imagine, while maintaining awareness, that the characteristics of the unpleasant experience change into those of the pleasant sensation. Imagine the color of the painful experience shifting to green if the pleasurable sensation had a green hue. Imagine the terrible sensation becoming soft if the texture of the good sensation were soft, and so on.

10. Be careful while transferring the positive traits of the pleasant sensation to the bad one.
11. Now examine the uncomfortable sensation. Has the feeling altered? Has the unpleasantness of this sensation increased? If not, carry on with this meditation.
12. This concludes the meditation.

Day 23

Experience Freedom

The majority of meditation methods recommend finding a comfortable seat and maintaining an upright posture. Learning to be accepting of all situations and to let go of control is one of the cornerstones of meditation. The body is the same way. You will listen to your body during this meditation and give it entire freedom to move or position itself as it pleases.

1. Sit down and make yourself comfortable and let yourself relax.
2. Close your eyes, pay attention to your breathing, and relax.
3. Ignore the advice your mother gave you about sitting upright. Allow your body to sag if it wants to. Give your body the freedom to do as it pleases.
4. Focus your attention on your body and its feelings. Keep your awareness in a relaxed state and avoid thinking too much.

Simply pay attention to your body's sensations and any signals it may be sending you. 5. This concludes the meditation. Feel free to give yourself as much time as you need to listen to your body.

Day 24

Our emotions help us determine whether we are growing closer to or further away from our integrity as human beings. We can't trust ourselves when we can't trust our feelings. In the next meditation, we'll pay attention to how our focus affects our feelings and bodily sensations.

1. Take a seat, close your eyes, and unwind.
2. Permit yourself to go into silence and pay attention to any internal ideas, feelings, emotions, or sensations. Allow each of these things to come to your attention.
3. Please consider a circumstance that is now making you feel uneasy, worried, or hurt. Allow yourself to concentrate on it when you find one of these circumstances. Imagine the sensation happening again.
4. As you concentrate on the circumstance, pay attention to any emotions that surface. Allow the emotions to come to you naturally. Keep in mind that your emotions are like a compass and are trying to tell you something.

They are directing your movement toward or away from the object of your attention. We can tell that we are on the right path and acting under our sense of integrity when we make choices, take actions, or concentrate on things that make us feel good.

On the other hand, when we feel unpleasant emotions, we are going through circumstances that are at odds with our sense of integrity. 5. At this point, ask yourself: "What can I do, believe in, or concentrate on to feel better about this circumstance?" Should you make a decision right now? Do you require letting go of anything? Do you need to analyze your reasoning? Do you require some personal time? Do you need to put others at risk?

5. Ask yourself questions over and over again until you find a solution that makes you feel relieved, at ease, or at peace.
6. When you identify a course of action for the problem that feels right to you, believe that this is the right choice for you. For you right now, your feelings are 100 percent true and trustworthy. Honor your sentiments as well if they alter your solution or the circumstance.
7. Be careful not to mistake your opinions or beliefs with your feelings. Your thoughts and opinions are not as trustworthy as your feelings.
8. It's also acceptable if you are unable to come up with a way to cheer yourself up. Permit

yourself to hang on to the emotion. Offer your complete acceptance of your feelings. Being at peace with our emotions and accepting them is a sign of integrity and self-love.

9. The meditation has come to an end. Please stay as long as you like in your stillness.

Day 25

Emotional Transformation

If you have a strong negative emotion that has been lingering inside of you, this activity will require you to take a more active part than in the last exercise. I advise you to read this meditation thoroughly before beginning to use it. Alternately, record it on audio tape and listen to it while performing this exercise.

Act as follows:

1. Take a seat and become comfy.
2. Shut your eyes and take a moment to unwind.
3. Pay close attention to your breath as it enters and leaves your body, concentrating on the feelings you have with each inhalation and exhalation.
4. Relive a memory that will trigger a negative emotion if you are not already feeling one. Consider a bad event you've had in the past or are presently going through.
5. Recognize the negative emotion when it manifests.
6. Examples include hostility, fear, worry, grief, etc.
7. After you've determined what feeling it is, describe how it feels. Be mindful that you should not describe how the feeling makes you feel, only how it feels. Use the term "It feels like________?" in your response to avoid slipping into this trap.

Here are a few instances:

"I feel like it's suffocating me."

"I feel as though I want to flee."

"I feel numb after it,"

I feel like a boulder is stumbling over me.

1. Repeat this process with your response once you've described how the emotion feels. For instance, if I'm feeling angry, I may say, "I feel like my body is constricting," in response to the sensation.

    e. After that, I would ask again, "How does it feel when your body tightens?
    f. I might respond, "I feel like my body is hard," to that.
    g. I would continue by asking, "How does a hard body feel?"
    h. I would keep asking the same questions after each response I made until the negative emotion changed to a positive one.

Use the first description of the emotion that occurs to you when describing it. You can't do it wrong, so don't bother about trying. You will be on the correct track as long as you express the emotion's experience without becoming cerebral about it. You give a feeling of room to change every time you describe it. The emotion will eventually change into a pleasant emotion if you keep explaining it each time it changes. Using this method helps the emotion come full circle and heal.

Day 26

Giving up

Nothing you encounter in life is independent of who you are. Our internal senses of sight, feeling, sound, and taste are how we interact with the outside environment. These occurrences just spontaneously appear and disappear in the area of your awareness. What are you clinging to then? What are you attempting to regulate? The focus of the next meditation is on giving.

1. Take a seat, make yourself comfortable, and unwind.
2. You have the option to close your eyes for the time being.
3. Permit yourself to unwind while concentrating on your breath. Pay close attention to how your breath enters your body, moves through it, and then leaves it as you exhale.
4. Continue to breathe normally, without strain. Relax.
5. Permit yourself to reach a state of complete acceptance. Be completely open to whatever arises in your awareness.
6. Refrain from evaluating, judging, or analyzing anything you encounter.
7. Let go of any notions of what you ought to be going through.
8. Do not seek anything. Do not use your imagination. Make nothing at all. Simply watch.

9. Allow any unwelcome or uncomfortable ideas, feelings, or sensations to surface.

10. Permit all of your experiences to become conscious. Do not attempt to alter them. Do not attempt to swap them out for something more uplifting or cheerful.

11. You are powerless to make a mistake. Whatever you are going through, this experience is the correct one for you.

12. Let awareness just flow through experience. Simply watch.

13. You have nothing left to do. Nothing needs to be changed on your end. You have no reason to believe anything. Simply observe anything that comes your way.

14. This concludes the meditation. Allow yourself to remain in \ssilence for as long as you desire.

Day 27

Challenging Minds and Cultivating Freedom

Congratulations if you completed every exercise in the preceding chapters. It demonstrates your commitment to altering how you see life and your receptivity to novel concepts. It's possible that you had trouble understanding this book's contents.

If so, I advise you to read it again and perform the tasks until they begin to make sense to you. Not everything in this book needs to be understood. Additionally, you do not need to complete all of the exercises successfully to benefit fully from this book. I want you to think about several key points when you reread this book, which I hope you do.

Everything in this book that has been written is something you already know. The only distinction between what is detailed in this book and what we often experience is that we typically ascribe our experience to a function of the environment or a function within ourselves.

If I am stuck in traffic and start to get upset, I will likely blame all the other cars on the road and my mounting annoyance. I consider myself a victim of my circumstances because I perceive myself as a distinct thing. After all, my experience of getting stuck in traffic was caused by external factors that were beyond my control. I shouldn't be surprised that I'm frustrated.

The viewpoint I've attempted to present to you in this book suggests a vastly different worldview. All of the items in my area of awareness, including the traffic jam and my view of myself, include thoughts, feelings, and sensations.

Every experience that I may have is taken in by awareness. That awareness is the essence of who I truly am. This is the subject of all that has been written in this book.

It's okay if this viewpoint looks overly harsh. I hope you will continue your investigation if any part of this book speaks to you. Since the moment of our birth, you and I have been living under the social conditioning of the culture. The generations before that were similarly brainwashed.

Neither our perception of the world nor our perception of ourselves is flawed. Our difficulty arises when we confine ourselves to this viewpoint and fail to recognize our genuine potential, which is limitless. You are more than your mind can comprehend, in actuality!

You should practice the activities in this book that seem right for you and study any sections of this book that you may still be unsure about for the reasons already mentioned. You'll probably need to reread this book if you didn't already understand metaphysics because there was a lot of information in it.

I'd like to leave you with one more thing before I go. The tale of the farmer who was staring at the moon was told in the introduction. Avoid mistaking the information in this book for what you are looking for, which is increased awareness. Everything you ultimately want is already inside of you and always has been. Just my technique of pointing to it is in this book.

www.ingramcontent.com/pod-product-compliance
Lightning Source LLC
LaVergne TN
LVHW041342200726

843509LV00009B/823